Pocket Prayers for Moms

Pocket Prayers for Moms

40 SIMPLE PRAYERS
THAT BRING PEACE AND REST

MAX LUCADO
WITH ANDREA LUCADO

THOMAS NELSON
Since 1798

Published in Nashville, Tennessee, by Thomas Nelson, a division of HarperCollins Christian Publishing, Inc.

Thomas Nelson titles may be purchased in bulk for educational, business, fund-raising, or sales promotional use. For information please e-mail SpecialMarkets@ ThomasNelson.com.

Unless otherwise noted, Scripture quotations are taken from the New King James Version®. © 1982 by Thomas Nelson. Used by permission. All rights reserved.

Other Scripture references are from the following sources: New Century Version® (NCV). © 2005 by Thomas Nelson. Used by permission. All rights reserved. Holy Bible, New International Version®, NIV® (NIV). © 1973, 1978, 1984, 2011 by Biblica, Inc.™ Used by permission of Zondervan. All rights reserved worldwide. www.zondervan.com. Holy Bible, New Living Translation (NLT). © 1996, 2004, 2007. Used by permission of Tyndale House Publishers, Inc., Wheaton, Illinois 60189. All rights reserved.

ISBN: 978-0-7180-4168-7 (TP)
ISBN: 978-0-7180-7739-6 (HC)
ISBN: 978-0-7180-7830-0 (eBook)

Library of Congress Control Number: 2015956800

Printed in Thailand
23 24 25 RRDA 8 7 6

www.thomasnelson.com

The Pocket Prayer

Hello, my name is Max. I'm a recovering prayer wimp. I doze off when I pray. My thoughts zig, then zag, then zig again. Distractions swarm like gnats on a summer night. If attention deficit disorder applies to prayer, I am afflicted. When I pray, I think of a thousand things I need to do. I forget the one thing I set out to do: pray.

Some people excel in prayer. They inhale heaven and exhale God. They are the SEAL Team Six of intercession. They would rather pray than sleep. Why is it that I sleep when I pray? They belong to the PGA: Prayer Giants Association. I am a card-carrying member of the PWA: Prayer Wimps Anonymous.

Can you relate? It's not that we don't pray at all. We all pray some.

On tearstained pillows we pray.

In grand liturgies we pray.

At the sight of geese in flight, we pray.

Quoting ancient devotions, we pray.

We pray to stay sober, centered, or solvent. We pray when the lump is deemed malignant. When the money runs out before the month does. When the unborn baby hasn't kicked in a while. We all pray . . . some.

But wouldn't we all like to pray . . .

More?

Better?

Deeper?

Stronger?

With more fire, faith, or fervency?

Yet we have kids to feed, bills to pay, deadlines to

meet. The calendar pounces on our good intentions like a tiger on a rabbit. We want to pray, but *when*?

We want to pray, but *why*? We might as well admit it. Prayer is odd, peculiar. Speaking into space. Lifting words into the sky. We can't even get the cable company to answer us, yet God will? The doctor is too busy, but God isn't? We have our doubts about prayer.

And we have our checkered history with prayer: unmet expectations, unanswered requests. We can barely genuflect for the scar tissue on our knees. God, to some, is the ultimate heartbreaker. Why keep tossing the coins of our longings into a silent pool? He jilted me once . . . but not twice.

Oh, the peculiar puzzle of prayer.

We aren't the first to struggle. The sign-up sheet for Prayer 101 contains some familiar names: the apostles John, James, Andrew, and Peter. When one of Jesus'

disciples requested, "Lord, teach us to pray" (Luke 11:1 NIV), none of the others objected. No one walked away saying, "Hey, I have prayer figured out." The first followers of Jesus needed prayer guidance.

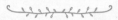

The first followers of Jesus needed prayer guidance. In fact, the only tutorial they ever requested was on prayer.

In fact, the only tutorial they ever requested was on prayer. They could have asked for instructions on many topics: bread multiplying, speech making, storm stilling. Jesus raised people from the dead. But a "How to Vacate the Cemetery" seminar? His followers never called for

one. But they did want him to do this: "Lord, teach us to pray."

Might their interest have had something to do with the jaw-dropping, eye-popping promises Jesus attached to prayer? "Ask and it will be given to you" (Matt. 7:7 NIV). "If you believe, you will get anything you ask for in prayer" (Matt. 21:22 NCV). Jesus never attached such power to other endeavors. "*Plan* and it will be given to you." "You will get anything you *work* for." Those words are not in the Bible. But these are—"If you remain in me and follow my teachings, you can ask anything you want, and it will be given to you" (John 15:7 NCV).

Jesus gave stunning prayer promises.

And he set a compelling prayer example. Jesus prayed before he ate. He prayed for children. He prayed for the sick. He prayed with thanks. He prayed with tears. He had made the planets and shaped the stars, yet he prayed. He

is the Lord of angels and Commander of heavenly hosts, yet he prayed. He is coequal with God, the exact representation of the Holy One, and yet he devoted himself to prayer. He prayed in the desert, cemetery, and garden. "He went out and departed to a solitary place; and there He prayed" (Mark 1:35).

This dialogue must have been common among his friends:

"Has anyone seen Jesus?"

"Oh, you know. He's up to the same thing."

"Praying *again*?"

"Yep. He's been gone since sunrise."

Jesus would even disappear for an entire night of prayer. I'm thinking of one occasion in particular. He'd just experienced one of the most stressful days of his ministry. The day began with the news of the death of his relative John the Baptist. Jesus sought to retreat with his disciples, yet a throng of thousands followed him. Though grief-stricken, he spent the day teaching and healing people. When it was discovered that the host of people had no food to eat, Jesus multiplied bread out of a basket and fed the entire multitude. In the span of a few hours, he battled sorrow, stress, demands, and needs. He deserved a good night's rest. Yet when evening finally came, he told the crowd to leave and the disciples to board their boat, and "he went up into the hills by himself to pray" (Mark 6:46 NLT).

Apparently it was the correct choice. A storm exploded over the Sea of Galilee, leaving the disciples "in trouble far away from land, for a strong wind had risen, and they were fighting heavy waves. About three o'clock in the morning Jesus came toward them, walking on the water" (Matt. 14:24–25 NLT). Jesus ascended the mountain depleted. He reappeared invigorated. When

he reached the water, he never broke his stride. You'd have thought the water was a park lawn and the storm a spring breeze.

Do you think the disciples made the prayer-power connection? "Lord, teach us to pray *like that*. Teach us to find strength in prayer. To banish fear in prayer. To defy storms in prayer. To come off the mountain of prayer with the authority of a prince."

What about you? The disciples faced angry waves and a watery grave. You face angry clients, a turbulent economy, raging seas of stress and sorrow.

"Lord," we still request, "teach us to pray."

When the disciples asked Jesus to teach them to pray, he gave them a prayer. Not a lecture on prayer. Not the doctrine of prayer. He gave them a quotable, repeatable, portable prayer (Luke 11:1–4).

When the disciples asked Jesus to teach them to pray, he gave them a prayer. Not a lecture on prayer. Not the doctrine of prayer. He gave them a quotable, repeatable, portable prayer.

Could you use the same? It seems to me that the prayers of the Bible can be distilled into one. The result is a simple, easy-to-remember, pocket-size prayer:

Father,

> *you are good.*

> > *I need help. Heal me and forgive me.*

> > *They need help.*

> > *Thank you.*

> > > *In Jesus' name, amen.*

Let this prayer punctuate your day. As you begin your morning, *Father, you are good.* As you commute to work or walk the hallways at school, *I need help.* As you wait in the grocery line, *They need help.* Keep this prayer in your pocket as you pass through the day.

When we invite God into our world, he walks in. And he brings a host of gifts: joy, patience, resilience.

When we invite God into our world, he walks in. He brings a host of gifts: joy, patience, resilience. Anxieties come, but they don't stick. Fears surface and then depart. Regrets land on the windshield, but then comes the wiper of prayer. The devil still hands me stones of guilt, but I

turn and give them to Christ. I'm completing my sixth decade, yet I'm wired with energy. I am happier, healthier, and more hopeful than I have ever been. Struggles come, for sure. But so does God.

Prayer is not a privilege for the pious, not the art of a chosen few. Prayer is simply a heartfelt conversation between God and his child.

Prayer is not a privilege for the pious, not the art of a chosen few. Prayer is simply a heartfelt conversation between God and his child. My friend, he wants to talk with you. Even now, as you read these words, he taps at the door. Open it. Welcome him in. Let the conversation begin.

Prayers for Time and Peace

1

Now may the Lord of peace Himself give you peace always in every way. The Lord be with you all.

2 THESSALONIANS 3:16

Father, you are wise and all-knowing. You allow all things to happen in your perfect timing.

Please give me peace in the midst of a busy season with my family. I feel pulled in so many directions by my kids' needs, my husband's requests, and my life.

Surround my family in this time. May your peace bring us all peace, and may you create a calm environment in our home.

Thank you that you have gone before us in this hectic time and for bringing order to the chaos when we need it most. Thank you for giving me time to hug my kids and show them what a precious gift they are to me.

In Jesus' name, amen.

2

The LORD will give strength to His people;
the LORD will bless His people with peace.

PSALM 29:11

*G*od, you are my strength during the hard times. Your grace is sufficient for me, and your power is made perfect in my weakness.

Today I feel spread thin and overcommitted. I don't have the strength in me to do what needs to be done. Give me the energy I need just for today. Give me time for rest and rejuvenation.

Protect my family as we run from one activity to the next. May my attitude be joyful, and may theirs be calm.

Thank you for going before our day and for your love and strength that sustain us.

In your Son's name I pray, amen.

You will keep him in perfect peace, whose mind
is stayed on You, because he trusts in You.

ISAIAH 26:3

Dear God, your ways are perfect. Your will is good. You deserve all praise.

You have promised perfect peace to those who focus on you. Help me to keep my thoughts on you. When I rush ahead to the next plan or responsibility, bring me back to you and your goodness.

Help my children to fix their eyes on you when they experience fear or anxiety. Show them who you are, and grow their trust in you.

I am grateful for the gift of peace we have in you. Thank you for the example of faith that I see in my children's lives.

In your precious name I pray, amen.

4

A man's heart plans his way, but the LORD directs his steps.

Father, you are above time. You know what will happen before it happens. You are the creator and ruler of all.

Steady my heart today as I make to-do lists. Direct my steps. Do not let me be overcome by anxiety and fear.

Direct the steps of my family today as well. Show them that your way truly is the best way, and give them a desire to do your will.

Thank you for your steadfast love. Thank you for giving me time to play with my children and for the joy that it brings to us all. I'm so grateful for their laughter and hugs.

In your name I pray, amen.

5

For the kingdom of God is . . . righteousness and
peace and joy in the Holy Spirit. For he who serves
Christ in these things is acceptable to God.

ROMANS 14:17–18

My father in heaven, only you deserve all glory and praise. You are my source of joy, peace, and love.

I so often make my own schedule and try to be the ruler of my calendar. Point me toward the things that please you. I want to draw near to you, God, and to do what is right in your eyes.

May my children serve you today. Do not let distractions or the Enemy get in the way of their focus on you.

I am so grateful that I am not in charge of my own life. Thank you for your constant guidance.

In Jesus' name, amen.

6

So teach us to number our days, that we
may gain a heart of wisdom.

PSALM 90:12

Heavenly Father, only you know the number of my days. In your infinite wisdom you have a plan for each of your children, including me and my children.

In this busy season remind me to live each day as if it's my last. Don't let me take a single moment for granted. May each of my actions be intentional during this time.

Be with my children today, Lord. Do not let them coast through this life, but instead give them an excitement for it and a deep joy that comes from you.

Thank you for caring about us and how we spend each day here on earth.

In Jesus' name I pray, amen.

7

Commit your works to the LORD, and
your thoughts will be established.

PROVERBS 16:3

God, you are a God who listens to his people. You hear when we call on you, and you don't ignore us.

Steady my thoughts today. My life feels so busy, and I have not had time to slow down. My mind is racing. Help me be focused in this moment.

Protect my kids' thoughts today. Do not let them be filled with worry or fear but rather with your love and assurance.

Thank you for listening to me when I speak and for the confidence that your love gives me and my family.

In the precious name of your Son, I pray, amen.

Prayers for Protection and Surrender

8

These things I have spoken to you, that in Me you may have peace. In the world you will have tribulation; but be of good cheer, I have overcome the world.

JOHN 16:33

Father in heaven, you cast out all fear with your perfect love. I am amazed by the perfect peace you bring to me.

Today I am worried about my children. Temptations surround them at school, with friends, online. Sometimes I feel helpless. Give me wisdom, and help me release them confidently to your care.

Protect my children today while they go about their activities. Protect them from evil and temptation. Hold them in your hands.

Thank you that even when I fear, I can trust in you. Thank you that I can rest in you.

In Jesus' name, amen.

9

Come to Me, all you who labor and are heavy laden, and I will give you rest. Take My yoke upon you and learn from Me, for I am gentle and lowly in heart, and you will find rest for your souls. For My yoke is easy and My burden is light.

MATTHEW 11:28-30

Dear God, you hold the entire world in your hands. There is no limit to your strength and power.

Be with me when I feel the weight of my children's struggles. Lift that burden from my shoulders.

And lift that burden from them too. Give my family strength to face the difficult times and hope even when the darkness feels overwhelming.

I'm especially thankful for the wisdom of older women who have walked this path before me. Their insights help point me to you in every circumstance. Thank you for placing mentors in my life who lift me up.

In your powerful name I pray, amen.

10

And who is he who will harm you if you become
followers of what is good? But even if you should
suffer for righteousness' sake, you are blessed.

1 PETER 3:13-14

Father, no evil can defeat you. No problem is too big for you. You see and know all.

Help me today, Lord. It is hard to let go of worry and fear for my kids. I am afraid of what could happen to them. Give me peace when anxiety surfaces.

Keep the evil one far from my loved ones today. Do not let him take a single ounce of joy or happiness from them.

Thank you for my suffering, for I know even in suffering that you are drawing me closer to you.

In Jesus' name, amen.

11

And Moses said to the people, "Do not be afraid.
Stand still, and see the salvation of the LORD,
which He will accomplish for you today."

EXODUS 14:13

40

God, you are a mighty warrior. You fight battles every day that I cannot see, and you are always victorious.

I need you to fight for me today. I feel weak, and I doubt when I know I should trust. I need faith that my family will be taken care of. The troubles we face seem so dark. Overcome my fear with your victory.

Fight for my family today, Father. When they feel sad or afraid or believe the problem is too big, show them how you will overcome.

Thank you that the battles belong to you, for you are capable and I am not.

In your name I pray this, amen.

12

The LORD is good, a stronghold in the day of
trouble; and He knows those who trust in Him.

NAHUM 1:7

Father, you are good. You are righteous, and you are worthy.

Help me when I doubt your goodness. Having children makes me aware of all the evil in the world, and it makes me afraid for my kids. Teach me how to trust in your unfailing goodness.

Be a stronghold for my family in times of trouble. Lift them up, and teach them to depend on your strength and not their own.

Thank you for being a steady rock and strong foundation for each of us today.

In the name of Jesus, who is my refuge, amen.

13

We are hard-pressed on every side, yet not crushed;

we are perplexed, but not in despair;

persecuted, but not forsaken;

struck down, but not destroyed.

2 CORINTHIANS 4:8–9

Dear God, you are bigger than my problems, worries, and fears. You are stronger than anything that could come against me or my family.

Give me strength today, Father. It feels as if everyone in my family is going through a hard time right now. Remind me that I am not forsaken and that you are on my side.

Remind my family of your promise that even when hard times come, they will not be destroyed. Even when they feel persecuted, you are with them.

Thank you that you walk beside me through every trial I face and have promised to bring me through it.

In Christ's name, amen.

14

But the Lord is faithful, who will establish

you and guard you from the evil one.

2 THESSALONIANS 3:3

My Father in heaven, you are the beginning and the end. You have gone before me and provided for me in all ways.

Lord, I am concerned for my children as they grow older. Each year brings new challenges, and I can't always protect them. Release me from fear, and show me how to surrender them to you daily.

Be with my kids at school today. Be in their conversations and interactions with their friends and classmates.

Thank you for your faithfulness. You never leave us. You never forsake us.

In your name I pray, amen.

Prayers for Guidance and Clarity

15

God is not the author of confusion but of peace.

1 CORINTHIANS 14:33

Father, your love is perfect, and your ways are perfect. I cannot begin to understand the depths of your love and wisdom.

Help me to be wise. As my family needs to make decisions, give me clarity and peace. You are not a God of confusion, so I want to hear your voice alone.

Please bring peace to my children as they make choices. Keep them far from confused thoughts and close to your perfect peace.

Thank you for direction and guidance. You always provide for us.

In the name of my true Provider, amen.

16

Peace I leave with you, My peace I give to you; not as the world gives do I give to you. Let not your heart be troubled, neither let it be afraid.

JOHN 14:27

Dear Father, you are righteous and worthy of my praise. You are the one true God, and I am in awe of you.

Sometimes I struggle with how to parent my children. They need discipline, and they need love, and I don't always know how to balance those things. Show me the way in this.

Be with my children when they fight and disagree. Give them a godly love for one another and deeper understanding and appreciation for our family.

Thank you for the unexpected delights of motherhood. Thank you for morning snuggles and evening laughter and for being with us throughout the day.

In Jesus' name, amen.

17

Be strong and of good courage . . . do not fear nor be dismayed, for the Lord God—my God—will be with you. He will not leave you nor forsake you.

1 Chronicles 28:20

Heavenly Father, you are the Lord of all, the almighty God, and the everlasting one.

Be near to me when my family faces change. When nothing feels steady, it is hard on all of us. Give me strength and courage in times of transition.

Allow my family to see you leading the way. May they rely on you, especially when they feel uncertain.

I am so grateful that even when everything around us feels unstable, you are there. You are our rock. I thank you and praise you for that.

In Christ's name, amen.

18

For God has not given us a spirit of fear, but of power and of love and of a sound mind.

2 TIMOTHY 1:7

Father, you are all-powerful, all-knowing, and almighty. You can move mountains and do wonders beyond my imagination.

Be with me today when I begin to fear. Remind me that fear is not of you, and replace it with peace and love and a sound mind.

Walk closely with my family today as they go in their own directions. Don't let them be overcome by fear or doubt, but instead fill them with a sense of your love.

Thank you that I never have a reason to fear, for you have given me the strength to meet any challenge today.

In your name I pray, amen.

19

Let us therefore come boldly to the throne of grace, that we may obtain mercy and find grace to help in time of need.

Father, you hear every prayer, and you see every face. You care about your children, including me.

I'm asking today for clarity. I so often try to figure things out on my own, but right now I'll stop trying. I surrender my life to you.

As I surrender my life, I surrender my children's lives as well. They are yours. Help them approach you with boldness so that they can know your grace.

Thank you that you've promised help in my time of need.

In Jesus' name, amen.

20

That the God of our Lord Jesus Christ, the Father of glory,
may give to you the spirit of wisdom and revelation in the
knowledge of Him, the eyes of your understanding being
enlightened; that you may know what is the hope of His calling.

EPHESIANS 1:17–18

God, you are good. Evil trembles in your presence. It is no match for your power and for your love.

Sometimes I get lost in my role as a mother, feeling as if it is my only identity. Remind me today that my identity is found in you.

Remind my family that there is hope in your calling, that you have a plan for each of their lives, and that it includes loving others as you have loved each of us.

Thank you for the incredible privilege of parenting my precious children. What joy and love they bring to my life, and they give me a little glimpse into how you must love me.

In your name I pray, amen.

21

The entrance of Your words gives light;
it gives understanding to the simple.

Psalm 119:130

Father in heaven, you speak all things into being. You create life with your words, and they bring light to the darkness.

Lord, bring light to my darkness today. The future can feel scary and is filled with the unknown. When my mind strays to anxious thoughts, light a path back to clarity and peace.

May your light enter our household today and bring understanding. My kids are still learning to trust in you, and I don't want them to fear the future. Give them peace and clear direction today.

Thank you for answering my children's prayers. Thank you for the whispered words they say just before bed—so often funny and always heartfelt. Thank you for putting them in my life.

In Christ's name, amen.

Prayers for Love
and Marriage

22

*The mountains shall depart and the hills be removed, but My kindness shall not depart from you, nor shall My covenant of peace be removed," says the L*ORD*, who has mercy on you.*

$\mathcal{D}$ear Father, you stay true to your promises. You do not break your word, and your love is steadfast.

My marriage is under attack from the Enemy, and there are moments I feel too weak to fight for it. Give me strength in those times, and remind me of the promises you have made to your children.

Guard my husband's heart. Bring us closer to you and to each other. Give us a supernatural love for each other and for our children.

Thank you that you are the ultimate covenant maker and keeper.

In Jesus' holy name, amen.

23

There is no fear in love; but perfect love casts out fear.

1 JOHN 4:18

Heavenly Father, only your love is perfect. It never fails. It is always right. It casts out fear.

I need your love for my husband and for my kids. When I get busy or stressed, I don't always show how much I love them. Let your love flow through me to my family.

Love my husband and kids today in a way that is tangible to each of them. Allow them to feel it all around them. Cast out their fear with your perfect love.

Thank you that your love is unfailing even when mine fails. I'm so grateful for my husband and the father that he is. Help me show him that today.

In your name I pray, amen.

24

Now to Him who is able to do exceedingly abundantly above all that we ask or think, according to the power that works in us, to Him be glory in the church by Christ Jesus to all generations, forever and ever. Amen.

Ephesians 3:20-21

Father, you are able to do more than I could ever ask or imagine.

There are parts of my marriage that feel broken beyond repair. I ask for your restoration and your love to do more than I ever thought possible in our relationship.

Protect those around us who are affected by our struggles, especially our children. Surround them and give us discernment when we are speaking to them.

Thank you that you still perform miracles and that your love brings restoration to all generations. My children and their children are part of that promise, and I'm so thankful to see that playing out in their lives even now.

In Jesus' name, amen.

25

I say to you, if you have faith as a mustard seed, you will
say to this mountain, "Move from here to there," and
it will move; and nothing will be impossible for you.

MATTHEW 17:20

Dear God, you created the world from the highest of the heavens to the depths of the sea. You know each detail of your creation.

Grow my faith today, for it is weak. Marital problems and disagreements in our home make me weary. Move mountains in my heart. Move mountains in my family.

God, be with my husband today. Fill us both with peace and understanding for each other and for our children.

Thank you for still moving mountains and accepting my faith no matter the state of it. I'm grateful for my husband's understanding and support. I feel treasured when he protects me and cherished when he shows me just how much he loves me.

In Jesus' name, amen.

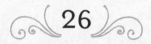

26

The LORD will fight for you, and you shall hold your peace.

EXODUS 14:14

*G*od above, you fight for us. You are the ultimate victor in every battle.

Remind me today, Father, that this battle isn't my own. When I get defensive with my husband or want to prove myself the winner of each argument, remind me that this is not my battle; it's yours.

Fight for my children today. When the Enemy tries to steal their joy, fight for them. When the Enemy tries to tell them they aren't good enough, fight for them.

Thank you for fighting on behalf of my family.

In your name I pray, amen.

27

Beloved, do not avenge yourselves, but rather give place to wrath; for it is written, "Vengeance is Mine, I will repay," says the Lord.

Romans 12:19

*G*od, your judgments are made in perfect love. I can't argue with your perfect will.

Set my eyes and my heart on you today. I am holding on to grudges against my husband, and I want to let them go. Teach me to leave my hurts with you.

Fill my husband with unexpected grace today for me and for our family. May his heart be soft toward you, and may your love refresh his spirit.

I give you thanks for your faithfulness. It is sure and strong and never ending.

In Jesus' name, amen.

28

*Now all things are of God, who has reconciled
us to Himself through Jesus Christ, and has
given us the ministry of reconciliation.*

2 CORINTHIANS 5:18

Father of light, you are in the business of reconciliation. You bring peace and hope even in the most desperate circumstances.

Give me the desire to reconcile with my husband when we argue. It is easier to remain angry and refuse to forgive. Bring us peace, and let your love overflow in my life.

Fill my husband and my kids with patience and grace. When they are at odds with each other, remind them that you can heal all wounds.

Thank you for the gift of grace and its power to transform relationships. Thank you for the work you've done already in my marriage and the joy you've given us. When my husband surprises me with an especially kind gesture, I marvel at your goodness in putting him in my life.

It's in Christ's name I pray, amen.

Prayers for
Healing and Safety

29

Be anxious for nothing, but in everything by prayer
and supplication, with thanksgiving, let your
requests be made known to God; and the peace of
God, which surpasses all understanding, will guard
your hearts and minds through Christ Jesus.

PHILIPPIANS 4:6-7

Father, you are the ultimate healer. Only you have the power to raise the dead to life and make all things new.

I need help trusting you today. When my child is sick, I feel helpless. Allow me to trust you with this burden.

I pray a bold prayer of healing for my child. Restore energy to him today, and give us evidence of improvement.

Thank you for caring about our illnesses, no matter how minor they are. Thank you that just holding my child brings us both comfort. These are precious moments that I'll always remember.

In Jesus' name, amen.

30

*Be strong and of good courage, do not fear nor be afraid
of them; for the LORD your God, He is the One who
goes with you. He will not leave you nor forsake you.*

DEUTERONOMY 31:6

Dear heavenly Father, you never leave us, and you never forsake us. You are our protector and our deliverer. I praise you.

Give me strength and courage today. There are children in my life who are sick, but we don't know the diagnosis yet, and we are so scared. Give us courage just for today.

My husband is trying to be strong for all of us right now. Give him rest and peace. Don't let him carry this burden alone.

Thank you for your promise to go with us and to go before us.

In Christ's name I pray, amen.

31

He was wounded for our transgressions, He was bruised
for our iniquities; the chastisement for our peace was
upon Him, and by His stripes we are healed.

ISAIAH 53:5

Father, you sent your Son as a sacrifice for us. You are a good Father, who cares for your children more than we could ever know.

I feel burdened today. It is so difficult to watch my child suffer when she is sick. Lift the burden from me, God, and give us rest from this illness.

Do not let my child's fear and pain prevent her from trusting you. She doesn't understand her suffering, but you do. I ask for quick healing and a full recovery.

Thank you that in the midst of even these difficult times, you bring moments of joy like the sweet delight of reading to my child and extra cuddle time.

It's in your name I pray, amen.

32

*Heal me, O LORD, and I shall be healed; save me,
and I shall be saved, for You are my praise.*

JEREMIAH 17:14

Father in heaven, you are good. There is no evil or impure thing in you. All good and perfect gifts come from you.

Remember me today. I need your saving grace and your healing. Fill me with it so that I can praise you.

I ask for healing for my children today. They need physical, spiritual, and emotional healing during this time in their lives. Be their comfort, Father.

Thank you for healing us ultimately by saving us. Thank you for the promise of eternity with you.

In Jesus' name, amen.

33

Now when the woman saw that she was not hidden,
she came trembling; and falling down before Him, she
declared to Him in the presence of all the people the
reason she had touched Him and how she was healed
immediately. And He said to her, "Daughter, be of good
cheer; your faith has made you well. Go in peace."

LUKE 8:47-48

*D*ear Father, just one touch from you can heal the sick and make the blind see. You perform miracles every day.

Help me in my unbelief today. When I start to doubt your power and your ability to heal, remind me of the story of the woman who touched you and was healed immediately. Her faith made her well. Give me a faith like that.

I ask for healing for the sick children I know. Perform a miracle, God. We need a miracle. When everyone tells us there is no cure, give us hope that you are the cure.

Thank you for the gentle way that you deal with your children and all the ways that you provide.

In your name I pray, amen.

34

*My son, give attention to my words; incline your ear
to my sayings. Do not let them depart from your eyes;
keep them in the midst of your heart; for they are life to
those who find them, and health to all their flesh.*

Dear God, your Word is good. It is life changing and life giving. It is steady and brings peace to all who listen.

Point me to scriptures today that are full of your promises. My heart aches for those who are sick and have been for so long. Bring me hope through your Word in a new way.

Comfort those who are ill. May they feel your arms around them as their bodies and hearts ache. Bring them healing, and allow them to rest well.

Thank you for giving us your Word so that we don't ever need to feel lost or alone.

In Jesus' name, amen.

35

O L<small>ORD</small> my God, I cried out to You, and You healed me.

P<small>SALM</small> 30:2

*G*ood Father, you hear all our cries. You care deeply about each and every one of your children.

I ask for healing today. You say if we seek, we will find; if we cry out, you will heal. Heal my sick child. Bring him relief and renewed energy.

Be with my friends who are also moms of sick children. May their suffering and their child's suffering draw them closer to you. Bring them miraculous healing.

I thank you for your mercy and faithfulness that never end. I thank you for friendships with other moms and the opportunity to support them. You've made us for community, and I am so grateful for the one you've given me.

In Christ's name I pray, amen.

Prayers for Grace
and Strength

36

*For by grace you have been saved through
faith, and that not of yourselves; it is the gift of
God, not of works, lest anyone should boast.*

EPHESIANS 2:8-9

Father, you alone can save. There is no one like you. You have redeemed the world.

Today I feel inadequate as a mother. I feel guilty for not doing more for my children and for my husband. Remind me that I am enough and that it is not me but Christ in me who makes me worthy.

Protect my family today when I can't be there for them. Surround my family with the kind of unconditional love only you can give.

Thank you that you are enough for me and that your grace will always be sufficient.

In Jesus' name, amen.

37

For all have sinned and fall short of the glory of God, being justified freely by His grace through the redemption that is in Christ Jesus.

ROMANS 3:23-24

Dear God, your love is unending and never failing, and your grace is a constant gift.

Some days I don't feel deserving of the privilege of being a mom. I forget things. I yell at my children. I neglect my husband. But I know I am made complete through your sacrifice.

Be with my husband today, Father. I pray that he will extend grace to me as you extend grace to me and that we will function as a team with you at the center.

Thank you for grace—the greatest gift of all—and the way it appears in my life. When I see your grace through my child's eyes, I'm refreshed and renewed. Watching my kids play reminds me of my own childhood and what you were doing in my life even then.

In your name I pray, amen.

38

Are not five sparrows sold for two copper coins?
And not one of them is forgotten before God. But the
very hairs of your head are all numbered. Do not fear
therefore; you are of more value than many sparrows.

Luke 12:6-7

*D*ear Father, you know each of your children by name. Nothing escapes your gaze.

There are days when I feel overlooked by my family. I feel underappreciated, as if they don't notice all the things I do for them each day. Remind me that your love is all I need. I am worthy simply because you created me.

I pray for other moms who also feel this way and for my friends who have forgotten who they are in you. May they feel loved and cherished.

Thank you for providing all the love and affirmation I need.

In Jesus' name, amen.

39

Not by works of righteousness which we have done,

but according to His mercy He saved us.

God, you are worthy of our praise and our gratitude. With everything in me, I praise you.

On days when I feel that I am at the end of myself, remind me that I don't need to be perfect. When I strive for perfection, I fall short. When I rely on you and not myself, I see how great you are. Teach me to focus on you.

Be with my kids today, and teach them that they must rely on you. Give them exactly what they need to get through today.

Thank you that I can rest in your promise of grace.

In Christ's name, amen.

40

You formed my inward parts; You covered
me in my mother's womb. I will praise You,
for I am fearfully and wonderfully made.

PSALM 139:13-14

Father, you are the creator of all. You knew me before I was born, and you know me intimately still.

My identity is so wrapped up in my job as a mom that when I fail, I feel as if I am a failure as a person. But you know every part of me and still accept me. Remind me of this throughout my day.

May my children know that they are loved not only by their parents but by you. May they find their worth in you and not in what others say about them.

Thank you for creating my family and loving them even more than I do. Thank you for the simple joys and the extravagant love that abound in our home. Thank you for surrounding me with such an amazing family.

In Jesus' name, amen.

About Max Lucado

More than 120 million readers have found inspiration and encouragement in the writings of Max Lucado. He lives with his wife, Denalyn, and their mischievous mutt, Andy, in San Antonio, Texas, where he serves the people of Oak Hills Church. Visit his website at MaxLucado.com or follow him at Twitter.com/MaxLucado and Facebook.com/MaxLucado.

About Andrea Lucado

Andrea Lucado is a freelance writer and Texas native who now calls Nashville, Tennessee, home. When she is not conducting interviews or writing stories, you can find her laughing with friends at a coffee shop, running the hills of Nashville or creating yet another nearly edible baking creation in her kitchen. One of these days she'll get the recipe right. Follow her on Twitter and Instagram, @andrealucado, or on her blog at AndreaLucado.com.

Discover Even More Power
in a Simple Prayer

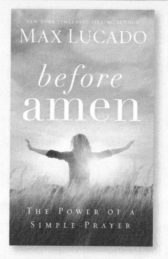

ISBN 978-0-7180-7812-6
$15.99

Join Max Lucado on a journey to the very heart of biblical prayer and discover rest in the midst of chaos and confidence even for prayer wimps.

Available wherever books are sold.

BeforeAmen.com

Make Your Prayers Personal

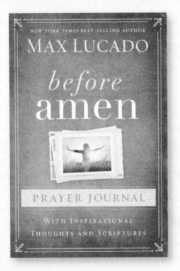

ISBN 978-0-7180-1406-3

$13.99

This beautiful companion journal to *Before Amen* helps readers stoke their prayer life. It features quotes and scriptures to inspire both prayer warriors and those who struggle to pray.

Tools for Your Church and Small Group

Before Amen: A DVD Study

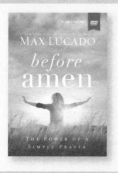

ISBN 978-0-529-12342-8

$21.99

Max Lucado leads this four-session study through his discovery of a simple tool for connecting with God each day. This study will help small-group participants build their prayer life, calm the chaos of their world, and grow in Christ.

Before Amen Study Guide

ISBN 978-0-529-12334-3

$9.99

This guide is filled with Scripture study, discussion questions, and practical ideas designed to help small-group members understand Jesus' teaching on prayer. An integral part of the *Before Amen* small-group study, it will help group members build prayer into their everyday lives.